CW00923152

Sunday Recipes

A Special Sunday Cookbook with
Savory Sunday Recipes for Breakfast,
Lunch, and Dinner

By
BookSumo Press

Published by
http://www.booksumo.com

ENJOY THE RECIPES?

KEEP ON COOKING
WITH 6 MORE FREE COOKBOOKS!

Visit our website and simply enter your email address to join the club and receive your 6 cookbooks.

http://booksumo.com/magnet

https://www.instagram.com/booksumopress/

https://www.facebook.com/booksumo/

LEGAL NOTES

Table of Contents

Bavarian Swedish Meatball 80

Beef Rolls of Bacon, Onions, and Pickles 81

Bavarian Empanadas 82

Ground Beef
Meatballs with Mushrooms

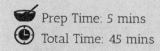 Prep Time: 5 mins
Total Time: 45 mins

Servings per Recipe: 5

Calories	389.2
Fat	17.7g
Cholesterol	95.7mg
Sodium	949.6mg
Carbohydrates	26.2g
Protein	30.1g

Ingredients

6 tbsp chopped onions
3 tsp butter
3 slices bread, torn into small pieces
3 tbsp milk
1 1/2 tsp prepared yellow mustard
1 tsp salt
3 -5 dashes black pepper
1 1/2 lb. lean ground beef
1 (8 oz.) cans mushroom stems and pieces, undrained

6 store bought gingersnap cookies, crushed with a rolling pin
1/2 C. water
3 tbsp packed brown sugar
1 1/2 tsp beef bouillon granules

Directions

1. Set your oven to 350 degrees F before doing anything else and lightly, grease a 2-1/2 quart rectangular baking dish.
2. In a skillet, melt the butter and sauté the onion till tender.
3. Transfer onion into a bowl with beef, torn bread, milk, mustard, salt and pepper and mix well.
4. Make about 29 (1-1/4-inch) sized meatballs.
5. Arrange meatballs into the prepared baking dish in a single layer.
6. In a small pan, add the mushrooms, gingersnaps, brown sugar, bouillon granules and water over medium heat and bring to a boil, stirring continuously.
7. Cook till sauce becomes slightly thick, stirring continuously.
8. Spread sauce over meatballs evenly.
9. Cover the baking dish and cook in the oven for about 35 minutes.

FULL
Bavarian Dinner (Country Vegetables and Beef Roast)

Prep Time: 20 mins
Total Time: 10 hrs 20 mins

Servings per Recipe: 8	
Calories	507.2
Fat	35.1g
Cholesterol	117.3mg
Sodium	303.6mg
Carbohydrates	9.7g
Protein	32.3g

Ingredients

3 lb. boneless beef chuck roast, trimmed
1 tbsp cooking oil
2 C. sliced carrots
2 C. chopped onions
1 C. sliced celery
3/4 C. chopped kosher-style dill pickle
1/2 C. dry red wine
1/3 C. German mustard
1/2 tsp coarse ground black pepper

1/4 tsp ground cloves
2 bay leaves
2 tbsp all-purpose flour
4 tbsp dry red wine
cooked pasta, of your choice
crumbled cooked bacon (optional)

Directions

1. In a large skillet, heat 1 tbsp of the oil and sear the roast till browned.
2. Drain off the grease.
3. In a small bowl, mix together the 1/2 C. of the red wine, mustard, pepper, cloves and bay leaves.
4. In the bottom of a slow cooker, place the carrots, celery, onions and 3/4 C. of the pickles and top with the browned roast.
5. Place wine mixture over meat mixture.
6. Set the slow cooker on Low and cook, covered for about 8-10 hours.
7. With a slotted spoon, transfer the meat and vegetables onto a serving platter and with a piece of foil, cover to keep warm.
8. Discard the bay leaves.
9. For gravy: transfer the liquid from slow cooker into a small pan and skim off extra fat.
10. In a small shaker, add 4 tbsp of the red wine and 2 tbsp of the flour and shake till well combined.
11. Place the pan of liquid on medium-high heat and stir in the flour mixture.

12. Cook till gravy becomes thick, stirring continuously.
13. Divide meat, vegetables and pasta onto serving plates.
14. Serve with a topping of the gravy.

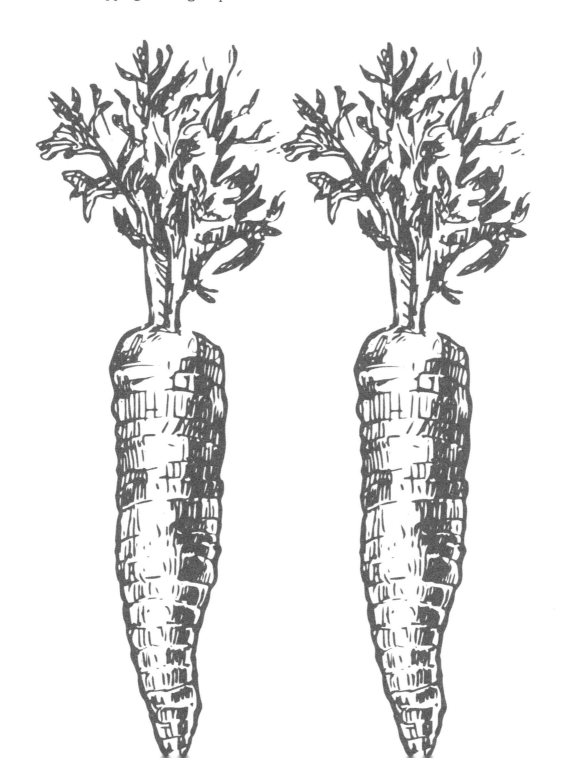

OLD
German Flank

Prep Time: 15 mins
Total Time: 1 hr 15 mins

Servings per Recipe: 4
Calories	507.2
Fat	35.1g
Cholesterol	117.3mg
Sodium	303.6mg
Carbohydrates	9.7g
Protein	32.3g

Ingredients

1 1/2 lb. flank steaks
1 potato, shredded
1 tbsp onion, chopped
1 tbsp green bell pepper, seeded and chopped
1 tsp pimiento, chopped
1 tsp parsley, chopped

kitchen string
3 tbsp canola oil
1 can onion soup
1 1/2 tbsp cornstarch
1/2 C. water

Directions

1. With a sharp knife, cut 1/4-inch deep slits in flank steak in a crosshatch pattern across both sides.
2. In a bowl, mix together potato, onion, bell pepper, pimiento, parsley and salt.
3. Place potato mixture over meat and roll up. With a kitchen string, tie the roll to secure the filling.
4. In a heavy non-stick skillet, heat the oil on medium-high heat and sear the steak roll for about 2 minutes per side.
5. Discard the drippings from pan.
6. Add the onion soup and stir to combine.
7. Reduce the heat to very low and simmer, covered for about 1 1/2 hours.
8. Transfer roll onto a serving platter.
9. Transfer the pan juices into a glass bowl and add enough water to equal 1 C.
10. In another small bowl, dissolve cornstarch into 1/2 cup of the water.
11. In a pan, add the cornstarch mixture and pan juices over medium heat and cook till thick, stirring continuously.
12. Cut the meat roll into 1-inch slices crosswise.
13. Serve with a topping of the sauce.

Bavarian
Sauerkraut Sausage Stir Fry

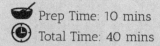

Prep Time: 10 mins
Total Time: 40 mins

Servings per Recipe: 4
Calories   542.2
Fat   31.5g
Cholesterol   74.7mg
Sodium   1900.4mg
Carbohydrates   45.1g
Protein   17.8g

Ingredients

1 lb. kielbasa, sliced
1 tbsp chopped onion
1 clove garlic, minced
1 C. sauerkraut, rinsed
2 C. water
1 C. rice, uncooked
2 tsp prepared mustard

2 tsp Worcestershire sauce
1 tsp salt
2 tsp caraway seeds
1/8 tsp pepper
1/8 tsp nutmeg

Directions

1. Heat a large skillet and cook the kielbasa till browned.
2. Stir in the onion and garlic and sauté till tender.
3. Stir in the remaining ingredients and bring to a boil.
4. Reduce the heat and simmer, covered for about 30 minutes.

OLD
German Rump Roast

🍳 Prep Time: 15 mins
🕐 Total Time: 9 hrs 15 mins

Servings per Recipe: 8
Calories	32.7
Fat	0.5g
Cholesterol	0.0mg
Sodium	220.1mg
Carbohydrates	5.0g
Protein	0.9g

Ingredients

1 boneless beef rump (3 lb.)
3 tbsp stone ground mustard
1 tbsp creamy horseradish sauce
1 (7/8 oz.) package brown gravy mix
1/2 C. beer

1/2 C. water
3 tbsp all-purpose flour
1 tbsp chopped fresh chives

Directions

1. Grease a 3 1/2-4 quart slow cooker with the cooking spray.
2. In small bowl, add the mustard, horseradish sauce and gravy mix and mix well.
3. In the slow cooker, place the beef roast and top with the mustard mixture evenly.
4. Carefully, place the beer around the roast.
5. Set the slow cooker on Low and cook, covered for about 9-10 hours.
6. with a slotted spoon, transfer the roast onto a serving platter and with a piece of the foil, cover the late to keep warm.
7. In a 2 quart pan, dissolve flour in the water over medium-high heat.
8. Add the cooking juices from slow cooker and bring to a boil, stirring continuously.
9. Stir in the chives.
10. Cut the beef into desired sized slices and serve alongside the gravy.

Countryside
Quinoa

Prep Time: 20 mins
Total Time: 45 mins

Servings per Recipe: 3
Calories	303 kcal
Fat	17.1 g
Carbohydrates	33g
Protein	6.2 g
Cholesterol	0 mg
Sodium	506 mg

Ingredients

1/2 C. quinoa, rinsed and drained
1 C. cold water
1/4 tsp salt
3 tbsps olive oil
1 celery rib, chopped
1 small onion, chopped
1 carrot, chopped
1 clove garlic, minced
8 almonds, coarsely chopped

1 small tomato, seeded and chopped
2 tbsps raisins
1/8 tsp salt
1/8 tsp ground black pepper
1/8 tsp dried thyme
1/8 tsp dried oregano
1 pinch coarse sea salt

Directions

1. Boil: salt, water, and quinoa.
2. Once boiling place a lid on the pot, lower the heat, and let the contents lightly boil for 17 mins.
3. Simultaneously stir fry the following, in olive oil, for 8 mins: garlic, celery, carrots, and onions.
4. Now add in: thyme, almond, oregano, tomatoes, pepper, salt, and raisins.
5. Cook the seasoned mix for 2 more mins.
6. Once the quinoa is finished stir it with a fork and then pour the quinoa into the carrot mix.
7. For 1 min stir fry the new mix to get the veggies evenly distributed throughout the quinoa.
8. When serving the quinoa top with some more sea salt.
9. Enjoy.

CARIBBEAN
Curry Quinoa

 Prep Time: 10 mins

Total Time: 1 hr 25 mins

Servings per Recipe: 4

Calories	162 kcal
Fat	2.4 g
Carbohydrates	31.1g
Protein	5.3 g
Cholesterol	1 mg
Sodium	553 mg

Ingredients

1 1/2 C. chicken stock
3/4 C. quinoa
1 1/2 tsps curry powder
1/4 tsp garlic powder
1/2 tsp salt

1/4 tsp black pepper
1 mango - peeled, seeded and diced
3 green onions, chopped

Directions

1. Boil, in a big pot: pepper, stock, salt, quinoa, garlic powder, and curry powder.
2. Once boiling place a lid on the pot, set the heat to low, and let the contents gently cook for 17 mins.
3. Let the quinoa loose its heat and add your onions and mangos.
4. Now stir everything to evenly distribute the fruit.
5. Enjoy.

Quinoa in Rome (Feta Cheese and Chicken Breast)

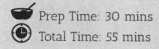 Prep Time: 30 mins
Total Time: 55 mins

Servings per Recipe: 4	
Calories	453 kcal
Fat	23.8 g
Carbohydrates	35.3g
Protein	23.8 g
Cholesterol	61 mg
Sodium	841 mg

Ingredients

1 C. rinsed quinoa
2 C. chicken broth
2 tbsps extra-virgin olive oil
2 garlic scapes, chopped
1 small onion, chopped
2 skinless, boneless chicken breast halves
- cut into strips

2 tbsps extra-virgin olive oil
1 zucchini, diced
1 tomato, diced
4 oz. crumbled feta cheese
8 fresh basil leaves
1 tbsp lime juice

Directions

1. Boil your quinoa in broth and once it's boiling place a lid on the pot and let the contents gently cook for 14 mins.
2. Simultaneously stir fry your onions and garlic for 7 mins, then add the chicken, and cook for 7 more mins.
3. Place the contents in a bowl, add in more olive oil (2 tbsps), and stir fry your tomatoes and zucchini for 10 mins.
4. Now add the chicken back in to the mix and top everything with: lime juice, basil, and feta.
5. Stir fry this mix until the chicken is fully done for about 8 to 12 more mins.
6. When serving your quinoa top it with some of the chicken.
7. Enjoy.

QUINOA
Chili

 Prep Time: 20 mins

Total Time: 1 hr

Servings per Recipe: 8	
Calories	126 kcal
Fat	4.9 g
Carbohydrates	17.5g
Protein	3.7 g
Cholesterol	0 mg
Sodium	154 mg

Ingredients

2 tbsps vegetable oil
1 C. uncooked quinoa
1 medium onion, finely chopped
3 cloves garlic, minced
1 small green bell pepper, chopped
1 (8 oz.) can tomato sauce
2 1/2 C. water

1 tsp chili powder
1/4 tsp garlic powder
1/4 tsp ground cumin

Directions

1. Stir fry, in veggie oil, for 9 mins: green peppers, quinoa, garlic, and onions.
2. Now add: cumin, garlic powder, and chili power.
3. Stir the spices in and then add: tomato sauce and water.
4. Get everything boiling and then place a lid on the pot and let the contents gently cook with a lower level of heat for 32 mins.
5. Every 5 to 10 mins stir your quinoa.
6. Enjoy.

Sirloin
Onion Egg Noodles

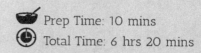 Prep Time: 10 mins
Total Time: 6 hrs 20 mins

Servings per Recipe: 8

Calories	684 kcal
Fat	16.9 g
Carbohydrates	90.6g
Protein	38.2 g
Cholesterol	146 mg
Sodium	902 mg

Ingredients

2 lb. sirloin tips, cubed
1/2 yellow onion, chopped
2 (10.75 oz.) cans condensed cream of mushroom soup
1/2 C. red wine
1 (1.25 oz.) package beef with onion soup mix

1 C. milk
2 (16 oz.) packages egg noodles

Directions

1. Heat a large skillet on medium-high heat and stir fry the beef and onion for about 5 minutes.
2. Meanwhile in a bowl, mix together the mushroom soup, wine, milk and soup mix.
3. Place the mixture in the skillet and bring to a simmer.
4. Reduce heat to low and simmer, covered for about 2 hours.
5. Reduce heat to its lowest setting and simmer, covered for about 4 hours.
6. In a large pan of lightly salted boiling water, cook the egg noodles for about 5 minutes.
7. Drain well.
8. Place the beef mixture over the noodles and serve.

THAI STYLE
Noodles

Prep Time: 30 mins
Total Time: 1 hr 5 mins

Servings per Recipe: 6	
Calories	695 kcal
Fat	32.9 g
Carbohydrates	70.5g
Protein	35.3 g
Cholesterol	187 mg
Sodium	383 mg

Ingredients

4 eggs
1 tbsp soy sauce
1 tbsp sesame oil
canola oil
1 (12 oz.) package extra-firm tofu, cubed
2 C. sliced fresh mushrooms
2 C. broccoli florets
1/4 C. chopped cashews
1 (10 oz.) package frozen shelled edamame (green soybeans)

1 (16 oz.) package egg noodles
1/2 C. unsweetened soy milk
1/2 C. peanut butter
1/4 C. reduced-fat coconut milk
1 tsp tahini

Directions

1. Set your oven to 350 degrees F before doing anything else.
2. In a bowl, mix together the soy sauce and eggs.
3. Heat a nonstick skillet on medium heat and cook the egg mixture for about 3-5 minutes.
4. Transfer the cooked eggs onto a cutting board and chop them.
5. In a large skillet, heat both the oils on medium heat and cook the tofu for about 8-10 minutes.
6. Transfer the tofu into a bowl.
7. In the same skillet, add the broccoli and mushrooms and cook for about 5-7 minutes.
8. In a baking dish, place the cashews and cook them in the oven for about 8-12 minutes.
9. In a microwave safe bowl, place the edamame and microwave it, covered for about 1-2 minutes.
10. In a large pan of lightly salted boiling water, cook the egg noodles for about 8 minutes.
11. Drain them well and keep everything aside.

12. In a large pan, mix together the remaining ingredients on medium heat and cook, stirring continuously, for about 2-4 minutes.
13. Add the noodles, tofu, chopped eggs, edamame and broccoli mixture and toss to combine.
14. Serve with a topping of roasted cashews.

HEARTY
Chili Noodles Bake

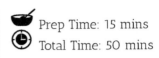

Prep Time: 15 mins
Total Time: 50 mins

Servings per Recipe: 6

Calories	510 kcal
Fat	20 g
Carbohydrates	49 g
Protein	27.6 g
Cholesterol	111 mg
Sodium	1129 mg

Ingredients

1 (12 oz.) package wide egg noodles
1 lb. ground beef
1 onion, chopped
3 cloves garlic, minced
2 (15 oz.) cans tomato sauce
1 (8 oz.) can tomato sauce
15 fluid oz. water

1 C. red wine
1 tbsp ground cumin
1 tsp dried oregano
1/2 tsp cayenne pepper
1 C. shredded sharp Cheddar cheese

Directions

1. Set your oven to 350 degrees F before doing anything else and grease a 14x9-inch baking dish.
2. In a large pan of lightly salted boiling water, cook the egg noodles for about 5 minutes, stirring occasionally.
3. Drain them well and keep everything aside.
4. Heat a large skillet on medium-high heat and cook the beef till browned completely.
5. Add the onion and garlic and stir fry them till the onion becomes tender.
6. Add the tomato sauce, wine, water, oregano, cumin and cayenne pepper and bring to a simmer.
7. Stir in the pasta and place the mixture into the prepared baking dish.
8. Top everything with the cheddar cheese and cook everything in the oven for about 20 minutes.

Noodles
& Shrimp Asian Style

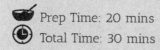 Prep Time: 20 mins
Total Time: 30 mins

Servings per Recipe: 6
Calories	322 kcal
Fat	6.3 g
Carbohydrates	49 g
Protein	15.1 g
Cholesterol	83 mg
Sodium	616 mg

Ingredients

1 lb. fresh Chinese egg noodles
2 tbsp olive oil
1/3 C. chopped onion
1 clove garlic, chopped
3/4 C. broccoli florets
1/2 C. chopped red bell pepper
2 C. cooked shrimp

1/2 C. sliced water chestnuts, drained
1/2 C. baby corn, drained
1/2 C. canned sliced bamboo shoots, drained
3 tbsp oyster sauce
1 tbsp red pepper flakes, or to taste

Directions

1. In a large pan of lightly salted boiling water, cook the egg noodles for about 1-2 minutes.
2. Drain them well and keep everything aside.
3. In a large skillet, heat the oil on medium-high heat, sauté the onion and garlic for about 1 minute.
4. Stir in the bell pepper and broccoli and stir fry everything for about 3 minutes.
5. Stir in the remaining ingredients and cook for about 3 more minutes.
6. Serve the noodles with a topping of the veggie mixture.

NOODLES
Russian Style

 Prep Time: 10 mins

Total Time: 20 mins

Servings per Recipe: 6

Calories	363 kcal
Fat	24.2 g
Carbohydrates	27.1g
Protein	9.9 g
Cholesterol	78 mg
Sodium	394 mg

Ingredients

1 (12 oz.) package wide egg noodles
1 (8 oz.) package egg noodles
2 C. sour cream
1/2 C. grated Parmesan cheese, divided
1 tbsp chopped fresh chives

1/2 tsp salt
1/8 tsp ground black pepper
2 tbsp butter

Directions

1. In a large pan of lightly salted boiling water, cook the egg noodles for about 8-10 minutes.
2. Drain well.
3. Add the butter and stir to combine.
4. Meanwhile in a bowl, mix together 1/4 C. of the cheese, sour cream, chives, salt and black pepper.
5. Place the mixture over the noodles and gently, stir to combine.
6. Serve immediately with a topping of the remaining cheese.

Roasted
Veggies Lasagna

Prep Time: 35 mins
Total Time: 1 hr 20 mins

Servings per Recipe: 10
Calories   410 kcal
Fat   14.6 g
Carbohydrates   48.4g
Protein   22.2 g
Cholesterol   38 mg
Sodium   1184 mg

Ingredients

olive oil cooking spray
2 zucchini, sliced
2 green bell peppers, cut in 1-inch pieces
1 (8 oz) package sliced fresh mushrooms
1 onion, cut into 8 wedges
1 tbsp chopped fresh basil
1 clove garlic, pressed
1/2 tsp salt

1/4 tsp ground black pepper
12 lasagna noodles
2 (28 oz) jars pasta sauce
1 (16 oz) package shredded mozzarella cheese
1 C. freshly shredded Parmesan cheese

Directions

1. Before you do anything set the oven to 400 F. Grease a casserole dish. Place it aside.
2. Lay the zucchini, bell peppers, mushrooms, and onion wedges on the baking pan. Top them with the garlic and basil then grease them with a cooking spray.
3. Sprinkle some salt with pepper on top. Cook them in the oven for 24 min.
4. Cook the lasagna noodles according to the instructions on the package until they become dente. Remove them from the water and place them aside.
5. Place a heavy saucepan over medium heat. Add to it the pasta sauce and bring to a simmer.
6. Get a mixing bowl: Stir in it the parmesan and mozzarella cheese. Place it aside.
7. Spread 1/3 C. of pasta sauce in the greased casserole dish. Top it with 3 lasagna noodles, 1/4 C. of the roasted veggies, 1/4 of the sauce and 1/4 C. of the cheese mix.
8. Repeat the process to make another 3 layers with cheese on top. Cook the lasagna in the oven for 24 min then serve it warm.
9. Enjoy.

ROASTED
Italian Cheesy Veggies

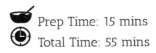

Prep Time: 15 mins
Total Time: 55 mins

Servings per Recipe: 6	
Calories	210 kcal
Fat	8.6 g
Carbohydrates	19.8g
Protein	13.4 g
Cholesterol	20 mg
Sodium	415 mg

Ingredients

2 russet potatoes, peeled and cut into
1-inch pieces
2 carrots, pared and cut into 1/2-inch
slices
1 tbsp olive oil
1 tsp dried basil
1 tsp dried oregano
1/4 tsp salt
1/4 tsp black pepper
1 large zucchini, cut into 1/2-inch
pieces

1 large red bell pepper, cut into 1/2-inch
pieces
2 cloves garlic, minced
2 C. Shredded Reduced Fat 4 Cheese
Italian Cheese
Fresh basil sprigs

Directions

1. Before you do anything set the oven to 400 F.
2. Toss the carrot with potato, a drizzle of olive oil, basil, oregano, salt and pepper in a large baking casserole.
3. Cook the veggies in the oven for 22 min. Add the bell pepper with garlic and zucchini then stir them. Cook them for another 22 min.
4. Toss the roasted veggies with cheese and bake them for 3 min. Serve your cheese roasted veggies warm.
5. Enjoy.

Roasted
Rutabaga and
Rooty Veggies

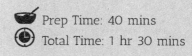

Prep Time: 40 mins
Total Time: 1 hr 30 mins

Servings per Recipe: 6	
Calories	99 kcal
Fat	4.8 g
Carbohydrates	13.8g
Protein	1.3 g
Cholesterol	0 mg
Sodium	67 mg

Ingredients

5 lb rutabaga, peeled and cut into 2x1/2 inch pieces
5 lb parsnips, peeled and cut into 2x1/2 inch pieces
5 lb carrots, peeled and cut into 2x1/2 inch pieces
3/4 tsp salt

1 1/4 C. vegetable oil
1/4 C. dried basil
salt and ground black pepper to taste
1 1/4 C. chopped fresh parsley

Directions

1. Before you do anything set the oven to 425 F.
2. Place a large saucepan over medium high heat. Stir in it 1/4 tsp of salt with rutabaga then cover it with water. Cook them until they start boiling.
3. Lower the heat to medium and put on the lid. Cook it for 6 min. Remove the rutabaga from the water and place it aside to lose heat. Repeat the process with the carrot and parsnip.
4. Get a mixing bowl: Toss the veggies with basil, a pinch of salt and pepper. Pour the oil into a casserole dish and heat in the oven for 6 min.
5. Toss the veggies in the casserole with the hot oil. Cook them in the oven for 12 min while stirring them often. Serve your roasted veggies warm.
6. Enjoy.

BALSAMIC
Roasted Veggies

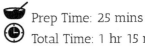 Prep Time: 25 mins

Total Time: 1 hr 15 mins

Servings per Recipe: 4	
Calories	1047 kcal
Fat	55.2 g
Carbohydrates	82.3g
Protein	51.2 g
Cholesterol	161 mg
Sodium	763 mg

Ingredients

cooking spray
4 beets, peeled and cut into 3/4-inch cubes
2 new potatoes, peeled and cut into 3/4-inch cubes
2 parsnips, peeled and cut into 3/4-inch cubes
2 turnips, peeled and cut into 3/4-inch cubes
1 rutabaga, peeled and cut into 3/4-inch cubes

2 tbsp olive oil
salt and ground black pepper to taste
1/3 C. vegetable broth
2 tbsp balsamic vinegar
1 pinch Italian seasoning, or to taste (optional)
1 (4 oz) package goat cheese, crumbled

Directions

1. Before you do anything set the oven to 450 F. Grease a baking pan with a cooking spray.
2. Get a large bowl: Mix in it the beets, potatoes, parsnips, turnips, and rutabaga with olive oil, salt, and pepper. Lay the mix on the baking pan.
3. Cook the veggies on the oven for 42 min.
4. Get a small bowl: Whisk the broth, balsamic vinegar, and Italian seasoning. Drizzle the mix all over roasted veggies then cook them for 12 min.
5. Toss the roasted veggies with goat cheese warm.
6. Enjoy.

Chicken
and Veggies Roast Skillet

Prep Time: 30 mins
Total Time: 2 hrs 25 mins

Servings per Recipe: 6	
Calories	754 kcal
Fat	45.6 g
Carbohydrates	36.2g
Protein	50.4 g
Cholesterol	146 mg
Sodium	388 mg

Ingredients

2 tbsp olive oil
4 red potatoes, cut into large cubes
1 (16 oz) package carrots, cut diagonally into bite-size pieces
1 stalk celery, cut diagonally into bite-size pieces
1 sweet onion, sliced - divided
1 (4.5 lb) whole chicken
salt and ground black pepper to taste
garlic powder, or to taste
1/4 C. margarine
1 large lemon, sliced
1 tsp minced garlic
1 stalk celery, cut into 3 pieces
1/4 C. margarine, cut into pieces
1 2/3 tbsp minced garlic

Directions

1. Before you do anything set the oven to 385 F.
2. Get a large bowl: Toss in it the potatoes, carrots, bite-size pieces of celery, and 3/4 of the sliced onion.
3. Season the whole chicken with garlic powder, salt and pepper.
4. Place the 1/4 of the sliced onion, 1/4 C. margarine, lemon slices, 1 tsp minced garlic, and large pieces of celery inside the chicken.
5. Lay the veggies in an ovenproof pan and place the chicken on top. Top the chicken and veggies with the rest of the margarine and 1 2/3 tbsp of garlic.
6. Cook the veggies and chicken roast for 1 h 50 min. Place a large piece of foil over the roast and allow it to rest for 12 min. Serve your roast Warm.
7. Enjoy.

AUTHENTIC
Austrian Pancakes

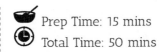

Prep Time: 15 mins
Total Time: 50 mins

Servings per Recipe: 6	
Calories	316 kcal
Fat	21.7 g
Carbohydrates	23.3g
Protein	7.5 g
Cholesterol	151 mg
Sodium	205 mg

Ingredients

1 C. all-purpose flour
1/4 tsp salt
2 tbsp sugar
1 C. milk
3 eggs

1 C. heavy cream
2 tbsp margarine

Directions

1. Set your oven to 325 degrees F before doing anything else.
2. In a bowl, mix together the flour, salt and sugar.
3. Add the milk, eggs and cream and mix till a smooth mixture forms.
4. In a cast iron skillet, melt the margarine.
5. Transfer the mixture into the skillet over the melted margarine evenly.
6. Cook in the oven for about 35 minutes or till a toothpick inserted in the center comes out clean.
7. Remove from the oven, and keep aside to cool till the pancake sets.
8. Serve with a drizzling of the maple syrup.

Traditional
Swedish Pancakes

Prep Time: 15 mins
Total Time: 30 mins

Servings per Recipe: 4
Calories	382 kcal
Fat	19.8 g
Carbohydrates	34.1g
Protein	16.5 g
Cholesterol	225 mg
Sodium	459 mg

Ingredients

4 extra large eggs, separated
1 C. all-purpose flour
1/2 tsp salt
2 tbsp white sugar
1 C. milk

3 tbsp sour cream
4 egg whites
3 tbsp vegetable oil

Directions

1. In a bowl, add the egg yolks and beat till thick.
2. In another bowl, sift together the flour, salt and sugar.
3. Add the flour mixture and milk into the egg yolks alternately and mix till just combined.
4. Stir in the sour cream.
5. In a third bowl, add the egg whites and beat till stiff but not dry.
6. Fold the egg whites into the mixture.
7. In a skillet, heat a small amount of the oil on high heat.
8. Add about 1 tbsp of the mixture into the skillet and tilt the pan to spread the mixture evenly.
9. Cook till the pancake browns from one side.
10. Flip the pancake and cook till browned from the other side.
11. Repeat with the remaining mixture.

EASTER
Brunch Pancakes

Prep Time: 15 mins
Total Time: 40 mins

Servings per Recipe: 8
Calories	360 kcal
Fat	19.5 g
Carbohydrates	31.2g
Protein	15.1 g
Cholesterol	89 mg
Sodium	792 mg

Ingredients

2 C. baking mix (such as Bisquick (R))
2 C. shredded Cheddar cheese, divided
1 C. milk
5 tbsp maple syrup
2 eggs

1 1/2 tbsp white sugar
12 slices cooked bacon, crumbled

Directions

1. Set your oven to 350 degrees F before doing anything else and grease a 13x9-inch baking dish.
2. In a bowl, add the baking mix, 1 C. of the Cheddar cheese, milk, maple syrup, eggs and sugar and mix till well combined.
3. Transfer the mixture into the prepared baking dish.
4. Cook in the oven for about 20-25 minutes or till a toothpick inserted in the center comes out clean.
5. Remove from the oven and top the casserole with the bacon and remaining 1 C. of the Cheddar cheese evenly.
6. Cook in the oven for about 5 minutes.

Turkish
Pancakes

Prep Time: 15 mins
Total Time: 1 hr 20 mins

Servings per Recipe: 8
Calories	86 kcal
Fat	3.5 g
Carbohydrates	10g
Protein	3.5 g
Cholesterol	48 mg
Sodium	124 mg

Ingredients

2/3 C. water
2/3 C. milk
2 eggs
1 tbsp vegetable oil
1/3 tsp salt

3/4 C. all-purpose flour

Directions

1. In a bowl, add the water, milk, eggs, vegetable oil and salt and beat till well combined.
2. Slowly, add the flour into egg mixture and beat till well combined.
3. Keep the mixture aside for about 1 hour.
4. Stir the mixture again.
5. Heat a lightly greased griddle on medium-high heat.
6. Add the mixture by large spoonfuls into the griddle and cook for about 2-4 minutes per side.
7. Repeat with the remaining mixture.

3-INGREDIENT
Fruit Banana Pancakes

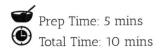

Prep Time: 5 mins
Total Time: 10 mins

Servings per Recipe: 2
Calories	93 kcal
Fat	2.7 g
Carbohydrates	14.9g
Protein	3.8 g
Cholesterol	93 mg
Sodium	36 mg

Ingredients

1 banana, mashed
1 egg
1 tsp arrowroot powder

Directions

1. In a blender, add the banana, egg and arrowroot powder and pulse till well combined.
2. Heat a griddle on medium heat.
3. Place half of the mixture into the griddle and cook for about 2-3 minutes per side.
4. Repeat with the remaining mixture.

Potato Soup
Russian Style

Prep Time: 20 mins
Total Time: 1 hr

Servings per Recipe: 12

Calories	167 kcal
Fat	7.7 g
Carbohydrates	21.2g
Protein	4.5 g
Cholesterol	23 mg
Sodium	928 mg

Ingredients

5 tbsp butter, divided
2 leeks, chopped
2 large carrots, sliced
6 C. chicken broth
2 tsp dried dill weed
2 tsp salt
1/8 tsp ground black pepper

1 bay leaf
2 lb. potatoes, peeled and diced
1 lb. fresh mushrooms, sliced
1 C. half-and-half
1/4 C. all-purpose flour
fresh dill weed, for garnish

Directions

1. In a large pan, melt the butter on medium heat and cook the leeks and carrots for about 5 minutes.
2. Add the potatoes, broth, dill, salt, pepper and bay leaf and cook, covered for about 20 minutes.
3. Remove from the heat and discard the bay leaf.
4. In a skillet, melt the remaining butter on medium heat and sauté the mushrooms for about 5 minutes.
5. Stir the mushrooms into the soup.
6. In a small bowl, mix the half-and-half and flour till smooth.
7. Stir into the soup to thicken.
8. Serve with a garnishing of fresh dill.

REALLY
Rustic Potato Soup

 Prep Time: 20 mins
Total Time: 50 mins

Servings per Recipe: 8
Calories	594 kcal
Fat	41.5 g
Carbohydrates	44g
Protein	12.6 g
Cholesterol	91 mg
Sodium	879 mg

Ingredients

1 lb. bacon, chopped, optional
2 stalks celery, diced
1 onion, chopped
3 cloves garlic, minced
8 potatoes, peeled and cubed
4 C. chicken stock
3 tbsp butter

1/4 C. all-purpose flour
1 C. heavy cream
1 tsp dried tarragon
3 tsp chopped fresh cilantro
salt and pepper to taste

Directions

1. Heat a large Dutch oven on medium heat and cook the bacon till browned completely.
2. Transfer the bacon onto a paper towel lined plate to drain.
3. Drain the bacon grease from the pan, leaving about 1/4 C inside.
4. Cook the celery and onion in reserved bacon drippings for about 5 minutes.
5. Stir in garlic, and cook for about 1-2 minutes.
6. Add the cubed potatoes and toss to coat and sauté for about 3-4 minutes.
7. Return the bacon to the pan and add chicken broth to just cover the potatoes.
8. Simmer, covered till the potatoes become tender.
9. In another pan, melt the butter on medium heat.
10. Slowly, add the flour, beating continuously.
11. Cook, stirring continuously for about 1-2 minutes.
12. Add the heavy cream, tarragon and cilantro and beat to combine.
13. Bring the cream mixture to a boil and cook, stirring continuously till the mixture becomes thick. Stir the cream mixture into the potato mixture.
14. In a blender, add about 1/2 of the soup and pukes till pureed.
15. Return the pureed soup to the pan and adjust the seasonings to taste.

Slightly Spicy Potato Soup

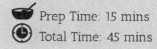 Prep Time: 15 mins

Total Time: 45 mins

Servings per Recipe: 6

Calories	366 kcal
Fat	29.6 g
Carbohydrates	16 g
Protein	10.4 g
Cholesterol	99 mg
Sodium	348 mg

Ingredients

2 tbsp butter
1 C. diced onion
2 1/2 C. peeled and diced potatoes
3 C. chicken broth
1 C. heavy cream
1 3/4 C. shredded sharp Cheddar cheese
1/4 tsp dried dill weed

1/4 tsp ground black pepper
1/4 tsp salt
1/8 tsp ground cayenne pepper

Directions

1. In a large pan, melt the butter on medium heat and cook the onion till softened.
2. Stir in the potatoes and broth and bring to a boil.
3. Reduce the heat and simmer, covered for about 15-20 minutes.
4. With an immersion blender, puree the potato mixture.
5. Place the pan on medium heat and stir in the cream, cheese, dill, pepper, salt and cayenne.
6. Bring to a low boil and cook, stirring continuously for about 5 minutes.

SIMPLE
Yukon Potato Soup

Prep Time: 15 mins
Total Time: 1 hr 15 mins

Servings per Recipe: 8
Calories	488 kcal
Fat	45.4 g
Carbohydrates	18.7g
Protein	3.7 g
Cholesterol	145 mg
Sodium	673 mg

Ingredients

1 C. butter
2 leeks, sliced
salt and pepper to taste
1 quart chicken broth
1 tbsp cornstarch

4 C. Yukon Gold potatoes, peeled and diced
2 C. heavy cream

Directions

1. In a large pan, melt the butter on medium heat and sauté the leeks for about 15 minutes.
2. In a bowl, mix together the cornstarch and broth.
3. In the pan, add the potatoes and broth mixture and bring to a boil.
4. Season with the salt and pepper.
5. Stir in the cream and reduce the heat.
6. Simmer for about 30 minutes.
7. Season with the salt and pepper before serving.

All You Need Is
Thyme Potato Soup

Prep Time: 20 mins
Total Time: 45 mins

Servings per Recipe: 6

Calories	338 kcal
Fat	10.8 g
Carbohydrates	51.6g
Protein	10.1 g
Cholesterol	31 mg
Sodium	857 mg

Ingredients

1/4 C. butter
1 large onion, chopped
6 potatoes, peeled and diced
2 carrots, diced
3 C. water
2 tbsp chicken bouillon powder
ground black pepper to taste

3 tbsp all-purpose flour
3 C. milk
1 tbsp dried parsley
1/4 tsp dried thyme

Directions

1. In a pan, melt the butter on medium heat and sauté the onion for about 5 minutes.
2. Meanwhile in another pan, add the potatoes, carrots, water and chicken soup base and bring to a boil.
3. Cook for about 10 minutes.
4. Season with the ground black pepper to taste.
5. Add the flour, stirring continuously till smooth.
6. Cook, stirring continuously for about 2 minutes.
7. Slowly, add the milk and stir well.
8. Reduce the heat to low heat and cook, stirring continuously till warmed completely.
9. Add the potato and carrot mixture, parsley and thyme and cook till heated completely.
10. Serve hot.

COUNTRY
Herbed Turkey Breast

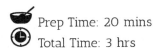 Prep Time: 20 mins

Total Time: 3 hrs

Servings per Recipe: 4
Calories	480.6
Fat	20.0g
Cholesterol	183.9mg
Sodium	167.8mg
Carbohydrates	10.6g
Protein	62.9g

Ingredients

1 frozen bone-in turkey breast (4-5 lb.)
1 pinch parsley, finely chopped
1 pinch fresh thyme, finely chopped
1 pinch fresh rosemary, finely chopped
1 pinch fresh ground black pepper

1 pinch paprika
2 oranges
1 lemon

Directions

1. Set your oven to 325 degrees F before doing anything else and arrange a rack in a roasting pan.
2. Thaw the frozen turkey completely.
3. Rinse the turkey breast under the running cold water and with the paper towels, pat dry.
4. In a bowl, mix together the parsley, thyme and rosemary.
5. Grate the oranges and lemon peel and keep the oranges and lemon aside.
6. Add the peels in the bowl with the herb mixture and toss to combine.
7. Rub the skin of the turkey with the herb mixture evenly.
8. Arrange the turkey breast onto the rack in the roasting pan.
9. Cut the oranges and lemon in half and squeeze their juices over the turkey breast evenly.
10. Season the turkey breast with the pepper and paprika.
11. Cook in the oven for about 2 1/2 hours, basting with the pan juices occasionally.
12. You can cover the turkey with a piece of the foil loosely to avoid over browning.
13. Remove from the oven and keep aside for about 15 minutes before slicing
14. Remove the skin from the breast.
15. Cut the turkey breast into desired slices and serve.

November's
Carrot and Garlic Turkey

Prep Time: 30 mins
Total Time: 33 mins

Servings per Recipe: 12
Calories	38.8g
Fat	256.2mg
Cholesterol	957.1mg
Sodium	12.5g
Carbohydrates	70.5g
Protein	38.8g

Ingredients

3/4 C. butter, softened
1 1/2 tsp poultry seasoning
2 tbsp garlic and herb sauce mix (recommended (Knorr)
1 1/2 tsp crushed garlic
1 (32 oz.) bags carrots
2 large onions, large dice
1 (32 oz.) containers low sodium chicken broth
12 lb. whole turkey, thawed if necessary

1 tbsp salt
1 tbsp pepper
3 (3/4 oz.) packets fresh herbs (sage, thyme and rosemary)
1 lemon, thickly sliced

Directions

1. In a bowl, add the softened butter, poultry seasoning, garlic herb sauce mix and crushed garlic and with a fork, mix till well combined.
2. Refrigerate, covered for about 15-30 minutes.
3. Set your oven to 450 degrees F.
4. In the bottom of a roasting pan, place the celery, carrots and half of the diced onions and top with the chicken broth.
5. Rinse the turkey under the running cold water and with the paper towels, pat dry.
6. With your finger, carefully loosen the skin around the entire turkey.
7. Cut the butter mixture into large pieces.
8. Place the butter pieces under the skin of the entire turkey.
9. Rub the remaining butter pieces over the outside of the skin and season with the salt and pepper.
10. Stuff the inside of turkey cavity with the remaining onions, fresh herb packet and lemon slices.

11. Arrange the turkey over the vegetables in roasting pan.
12. Transfer the roasting pan in the oven and set your oven to 325 degrees F.
13. Cook in the oven for about 1 hour.
14. Baste the turkey with the pan juices.
15. Cook in the oven for about 3 hours, basting with the pan juices after every 20 minutes.

Italian
Herb Turkey

Prep Time: 25 mins
Total Time: 4 hrs 45 mins

Servings per Recipe: 16
Calories	596 kcal
Fat	33.7 g
Carbohydrates	0.8g
Protein	< 68.1 g
Cholesterol	198 mg
Sodium	165 mg

Ingredients

3/4 C. olive oil
3 tbsp minced garlic
2 tbsp chopped fresh rosemary
1 tbsp chopped fresh basil
1 tbsp Italian seasoning

1 tsp ground black pepper
salt to taste
1 (12 lb.) whole turkey

Directions

1. Set your oven to 325 degrees F before doing anything else and arrange a rack in a large roasting pan.
2. In a small bowl, mix together the olive oil, garlic, rosemary, basil, Italian seasoning, black pepper and salt.
3. Rinse the turkey under the running cold water and with the paper towels, pat dry.
4. Remove the fat from the turkey.
5. With your fingers carefully, loosen the skin from the breast.
6. With your hand, spread a generous amount of the rosemary mixture under the breast skin and down the thigh and leg.
7. Rub the remaining rosemary mixture over the outside of the breast.
8. Arrange the turkey onto the rack in the roasting pan.
9. Add about 1/4-inch of water in the bottom of the roasting pan.
10. Cook in the oven for about 3-4 hours.

TURKEY
for Easter

Prep Time: 30 mins
Total Time: 4 hrs 45 mins

Servings per Recipe: 16
Calories	828 kcal
Fat	41.1 g
Carbohydrates	17.7g
Protein	92.1 g
Cholesterol	283 mg
Sodium	555 mg

Ingredients

1 (16 lb.) whole turkey, neck and giblets removed
1/4 C. extra-virgin olive oil
1 tsp salt
1/2 tsp ground black pepper
1 tsp ground thyme
1 C. honey

1/2 C. melted butter
2 tsp dried sage leaves
1 tbsp minced fresh parsley
1 tsp dried basil
1 tsp salt
1 tsp ground black pepper

Directions

1. Set your oven to 325 degrees F before doing anything else and arrange a rack in a large roasting pan.
2. Rinse the turkey under the running cold water and with the paper towels, pat dry.
3. Coat the turkey with the olive oil from the inside and outside.
4. In a bowl, mix together 1 tsp of the salt, 1/2 tsp of the pepper and thyme.
5. Season the turkey with the thyme mixture evenly.
6. Arrange the turkey onto the rack in the roasting pan.
7. Cook in the oven for about 2 hours.
8. In a bowl, add the honey, melted butter, sage, parsley, basil, 1 tsp of the salt and 1 tsp of the pepper and mix till smooth.
9. Remove the turkey from the oven and coat with the honey glaze evenly.
10. Cook in the oven for about 2 hours, coating with the honey glaze occasionally.
11. Remove the turkey from the oven and transfer onto a platter.
12. With a double pieces of the foil, cover the turkey loosely for about 10-15 minutes before slicing.

Roasted
Turkey of Classical Americana

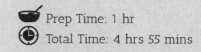 Prep Time: 1 hr
Total Time: 4 hrs 55 mins

Servings per Recipe: 16

Calories	942 kcal
Fat	70.1 g
Carbohydrates	4.6 g
Protein	68.7 g
Cholesterol	256 mg
Sodium	974 mg

Ingredients

2 tbsp kosher salt
1 tbsp ground black pepper
1 tbsp poultry seasoning
1 (12 lb.) whole turkey, neck and giblets reserved
2 onions, coarsely chopped
3 ribs celery, coarsely chopped
2 carrots, coarsely chopped
3 sprigs fresh rosemary
1/2 bunch fresh sage
1/2 C. butter
1 bay leaf

6 C. water
2 tbsp turkey fat
1 tbsp butter
1/4 C. all-purpose flour
3 C. turkey pan drippings
1/4 tsp balsamic vinegar (optional)
1 tbsp chopped fresh sage
salt and ground black pepper to taste

Directions

1. Set your oven to 325 degrees F before doing anything else.
2. In a small bowl, mix together 2 tbsp of the salt, 1 tbsp of the pepper and poultry seasoning.
3. Tuck the wings under the turkey and season the cavity with about 1 tbsp of the poultry seasoning mixture.
4. Reserve the remaining poultry seasoning mixture.
5. In a bowl, mix together the onion, celery and carrots.
6. Stuff the turkey cavity with about 1/2 C. of the vegetable mixture, rosemary sprigs and 1/2 bunch of he sage.
7. With the kitchen string, tie the legs together.
8. With your fingers carefully, loosen the skin on top of the turkey breast.
9. Rub about 2 tbsp of the butter under the skin evenly.

10. Spread the remaining butter over the outside of the skin evenly.
11. Season the outside of the turkey with the remaining poultry seasoning mixture.
12. Place the remaining onion, celery and carrots in a large roasting pan.
13. Arrange the turkey over the vegetables.
14. Add about 1/2-inch of the water in the roasting pan.
15. Place a piece of the foil over the turkey breast.
16. Cook in the oven for about 2 1/2 hours.
17. Remove the foil and baste the turkey with the pan juices.
18. Cook in the oven for about 1 hour.
19. Meanwhile for the stock in a pan, add the neck, giblets, bay leaf and water on medium heat and simmer for about 2 hours.
20. Strain the turkey broth and discard the giblets. (There should be at least 4 C. of stock.)
21. Remove the turkey from the oven and transfer onto a platter.
22. With a double pieces of the foil, cover the turkey for about 10-15 minutes before slicing.
23. In a pan, add about 3 C. of the pan juices.
24. Skim off the fat from the pan juices, reserving about 2 tbsp.
25. In a skillet, heat 2 tbsp of the turkey fat and 1 tbsp of the butter on medium heat.
26. Transfer the onions from the roasting pan into the skillet and sauté for about 5 minutes.
27. Stir in the flour and cook for about 5 minutes, stirring continuously.
28. Add 4 C. of the turkey stock and the reserved pan juices and beat till smooth.
29. Skim off any foam from the top surface.
30. Stir in the balsamic vinegar and simmer for about 10 minutes, beating continuously.
31. Stir in 1 tbsp of the chopped sage, salt and black pepper.
32. Serve the turkey alongside the gravy.

Georgia
Omelet

Prep Time: 15 mins
Total Time: 25 mins

Servings per Recipe: 3
Calories	345 kcal
Fat	26.8 g
Carbohydrates	8.9g
Protein	17 g
Cholesterol	397 mg
Sodium	647 mg

Ingredients

1 C. peeled, sliced peaches
2 tbsp lemon juice
4 slices bacon
2 tbsp water
6 eggs
1 tsp chopped fresh chives
1/4 tsp salt

1 tbsp white sugar
1/8 tsp ground black pepper
1 pinch paprika

Directions

1. In a bowl, mix together the peaches and lemon juice and keep aside.
2. Heat a large, deep skillet on medium-high heat and cook the bacon till browned completely.
3. Transfer the bacon onto a paper towel lined plate to drain and then crumble it.
4. Reserve 1 tbsp of the bacon grease in the skillet.
5. In a large bowl, add the water, crumbled bacon, eggs, chives, sugar, chives, salt and black pepper and mix till well combined.
6. Reheat the bacon grease on medium-high heat and cook the egg mixture till set slightly.
7. Arrange the peach slices over the egg mixture.
8. Reduce the heat to medium and cook, covered for about 1 minute.
9. Uncover and cook till set completely.
10. Sprinkle with the paprika and remove from the heat.
11. Keep aside to cool slightly before serving.

ASPARAGUS
Omelet

Prep Time: 15 mins
Total Time: 25 mins

Servings per Recipe: 1

Calories	537 kcal
Fat	39.2 g
Carbohydrates	11.2g
Protein	36.6 g
Cholesterol	421 mg
Sodium	938 mg

Ingredients

1 tbsp olive oil
2 eggs
1/4 C. milk (optional)
3 spears asparagus, trimmed and cut
into 2-inch pieces

1/2 C. sliced fresh mushrooms
1/3 C. green onions, chopped
1/2 C. grated Parmesan cheese

Directions

1. In a bowl, add the milk and eggs and beat well. Keep aside.
2. In a large skillet, heat the oil on medium-high heat and cook the mushrooms, asparagus and green onions for about 4 minutes.
3. Place thee egg mixture over the asparagus mixture evenly and reduce the heat to medium.
4. During the cooking, carefully lift the edge to allow the uncooked egg to flow underneath.
5. When the omelet is almost done sprinkle with the Parmesan cheese and cook till cheese is melted slightly.
6. Carefully, fold in half and serve.

Olives
Omelet

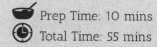 Prep Time: 10 mins
Total Time: 55 mins

Servings per Recipe: 6

Calories	287 kcal
Fat	21.3 g
Carbohydrates	4.5g
Protein	20 g
Cholesterol	341 mg
Sodium	904 mg

Ingredients

10 eggs
1/3 C. milk
1/2 tsp salt
4 dashes hot pepper sauce
1/2 lb. bacon - cooked, and chopped into bite-size pieces
1 (4 oz.) can black olives, drained

2 roma (plum) tomatoes, chopped
1/4 C. green onions, chopped
1/3 C. mushrooms, sliced
3/4 C. Colby-Monterey Jack cheese, shredded

Directions

1. Set your oven to 350 degrees F before doing anything else and grease an 8-inch square baking dish.
2. In a large bowl, add the milk, eggs, salt and hot pepper sauce and with an electric mixer, beat till frothy.
3. Add the bacon, mushrooms, olives, tomatoes, green onions and cheese and stir to combine.
4. Place the egg mixture into prepared baking dish evenly and cover with a piece of foil.
5. Cook in the oven for about 40-50 minutes.

CHEESY
Bell Omelet

Prep Time: 20 mins
Total Time: 1 hr

Servings per Recipe: 2

Calories	386 kcal
Fat	29.8 g
Carbohydrates	9.1g
Protein	21.7 g
Cholesterol	430 mg
Sodium	1158 mg

Ingredients

2 tbsp butter
1 small onion, chopped
1 green bell pepper, chopped
4 eggs
2 tbsp milk

3/4 tsp salt
1/8 tsp freshly ground black pepper
2 oz. shredded Swiss cheese

Directions

1. In a medium skillet, melt 1 tbsp of the butter on medium heat and cook the onion and bell pepper for about 4-5 minutes, stirring occasionally.
2. In a bowl, add the milk, eggs, 1/2 tsp of the salt and pepper and beat till well combined.
3. In another bowl, place the cheese and keep aside.
4. Transfer the onion mixture into a bowl and sprinkle remaining 1/4 tsp of the salt.
5. In the same skillet, melt remaining 1 tbsp of the butter on medium heat and cook the egg mixture for about 2 minutes.
6. With a spatula, gently lift the edges of the omelet and cook for about 2-3 minutes.
7. Sprinkle the omelet with the cheese and then, place the onion mixture in the center of the omelet.
8. Gently, fold one edge of the omelet over the vegetables and cook for about 1-2 minutes.
9. transfer the omelet onto a plate.
10. Cut in half and serve.

Mediterranean Stew

Prep Time: 15 mins
Total Time: 1 hr 40 mins

Servings per Recipe: 6

Calories	383 kcal
Fat	19.7 g
Carbohydrates	11.1g
Protein	25.3 g
Cholesterol	86 mg
Sodium	402 mg

Ingredients

1 cooking spray (such as Pam(R))
2 tbsps olive oil, divided
2 large onions, cut into 1/2-inch dice
4 cloves garlic, or more to taste, minced
8 chicken thighs, or more to taste, trimmed
2 C. dry white wine
2 (6.5 oz.) cans tomato sauce
1/2 tsp ground black pepper
1 lemon, juiced
1 drop hot pepper sauce (such as Tabasco(R))
1 pinch ground cinnamon

Directions

1. Coat a big pot with nonstick spray then add in 1 tbsp of olive oil.
2. Begin to stir fry your garlic and onions for 7 mins then place the mix to the side.
3. Add the rest of the oil and brown your chicken in it for 7 mins.
4. Combine in the wine and get everything boiling.
5. Once the mix is boiling reduce the heat to low and gently cook the chicken for 17 mins.
6. Now combine in the cinnamon, tomato sauce, onion mix, hot sauce, black pepper, and lemon juice.
7. Get the mix boiling again, set the heat to low, place a lid over on the pot, and gently cook the stew for 65 mins.
8. Enjoy.

MAGGIE'S
Rutabaga Stew

Prep Time: 20 mins
Total Time: 4 hrs 25 mins

Servings per Recipe: 15	
Calories	111 kcal
Fat	2.1 g
Carbohydrates	12.9g
Protein	10.7 g
Cholesterol	23 mg
Sodium	80 mg

Ingredients

1 tbsp vegetable oil
1 1/2 lbs chicken, diced
4 rutabagas, peeled and diced
4 medium beets, peeled and diced
4 carrots, diced

3 stalks celery, diced
1 red onion, diced
water, or to cover

Directions

1. Stir fry your chicken in veggie oil for 4 mins.
2. Now combine in: red onions, rutabagas, celery, beets, and carrots. Submerge the contents in some water and get the mix boiling.
3. Once the mix is boiling set the heat to low, and simmer the stew for 4 hrs.
4. Make sure you continue to add some water during the cooking time to keep the veggies simmering.
5. Enjoy.

Rustic
Venison

Prep Time: 20 mins
Total Time: 2 hrs 25 mins

Servings per Recipe: 6

Calories	353 kcal
Fat	8.5 g
Carbohydrates	25.7g
Protein	35.2 g
Cholesterol	120 mg
Sodium	542 mg

Ingredients

2 tbsps bacon grease
2 lbs venison, cut into chunks
1 onion, diced
2 cloves garlic, minced
1 tbsp tomato paste
1 tsp anchovy paste
3 tbsps all-purpose flour
1 C. red wine
1 C. beef broth

1 C. chicken broth
1 tsp ground thyme
2 bay leaves
1 lb small red potatoes, diced
4 carrots, diced
1/2 C. sliced mushrooms
1/2 C. frozen peas
1 pinch salt and ground black pepper to taste

Directions

1. Set your oven to 300 degrees before doing anything else.
2. Stir fry your venison, in bacon grease, in a large pot, for 7 mins, to brown it. Place the meat to the side.
3. Now begin to stir fry your onions in the oil for 6 mins then add in: anchovy paste, garlic, and tomato paste. Then add in flour over the mix and stir everything.
4. Add the chicken and beef broth, and the wine as well and get everything boiling.
5. Scrape the pan then add in the bay leaves and thyme.
6. Get the mix boiling again then add the venison.
7. Get the mix to a light boil with a low to medium level of heat and cook everything for 65 mins. Then add in the mushrooms, potatoes, and carrots. Place the stew in the oven for 60 more mins.
8. Enjoy.

UPSTATE
Chicken Stew

Prep Time: 20 mins
Total Time: 2 hrs 20 mins

Servings per Recipe: 6

Calories	275 kcal
Fat	2.3 g
Carbohydrates	41.8g
Protein	21.8 g
Cholesterol	43 mg
Sodium	435 mg

Ingredients

4 C. water
1 lb chicken tenders
3 carrots, cut into chunks
2 stalks celery, cut into chunks
2 potatoes, diced
1 sweet potato, diced

1 (15 oz.) can peas
1 (8 oz.) can tomato sauce
2 bay leaves
1 C. cooked rice

Directions

1. Get the following boiling: bay leaves, water, tomato sauce, chicken, peas, carrots, sweet potatoes, regular potatoes, and celery.
2. Once the mix is boiling set the heat to low and let the contents cook for about 2 hrs.
3. Now add the rice and let everything simmer for 20 more mins.
4. Enjoy.

Waffle IV (Ginger)

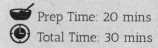
Prep Time: 20 mins
Total Time: 30 mins

Servings per Recipe: 4

Calories	177 kcal
Carbohydrates	29.7 g
Cholesterol	8 mg
Fat	4.1 g
Protein	6 g
Sodium	308 mg

Ingredients

1 tbsp butter, softened
2 tbsps molasses
1/4 C. liquid egg substitute
1/2 C. Kamut flour
1/2 C. whole wheat pastry flour
1 tsp baking powder
1/4 tsp baking soda
1/8 tsp sea salt
1 tsp ground ginger

1/2 tsp cinnamon
1/8 tsp ground cloves
3/4 C. boiling water, or as needed

Directions

1. Get a bowl, mix evenly: egg substitute, butter, and molasses.
2. Get a 2nd bowl, sift: cloves, whole wheat flour, cinnamon, baking soda and powder, ginger, and salt.
3. Combine both bowls with some water and flour. Mix until even.
4. Heat your waffle iron. Cover with nonstick spray.
5. Ladle batter onto the iron. Cook until crispy. Continue with remaining batter.
6. Enjoy.

CORNMEAL
Waffle

Prep Time: 10 mins
Total Time: 15 mins

Servings per Recipe: 5

Calories	415 kcal
Carbohydrates	46.3 g
Cholesterol	78 mg
Fat	21 g
Protein	10.3 g
Sodium	813 mg

Ingredients

1 C. all-purpose flour
1 C. stone-ground cornmeal
2 tsps baking powder
1 tsp baking soda
1/2 tsp salt
1/3 C. vegetable oil

2 eggs
2 C. buttermilk
1 tbsp oil, or as needed for greasing

Directions

1. Get a bowl, sift: salt, flour, baking soda and soda.
2. Get a 2nd bowl, mix evenly: buttermilk, veggie oil (1/3 C.), and beaten eggs.
3. Combine both bowls evenly to make batter.
4. Heat waffle iron and coat with nonstick spray.
5. Ladle enough batter to fill 75% of the iron's surface. Cook until golden. Repeat for all batter.
6. Enjoy.

Mediterranean
Waffle
(Garbanzo Beans)

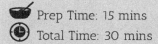

Prep Time: 15 mins
Total Time: 30 mins

Servings per Recipe: 4

Calories	210 kcal
Carbohydrates	38.7 g
Cholesterol	0 mg
Fat	2.1 g
Protein	10 g
Sodium	1471 mg

Ingredients

nonstick spray
2 (15 oz) cans garbanzo beans (chickpeas), drained and rinsed
1 medium onion, chopped
2 large egg whites
1/4 C. chopped fresh cilantro
1/4 C. chopped fresh parsley
3 cloves roasted garlic, or more to taste
1 1/2 tbsps all-purpose flour

2 tsps ground cumin
1 3/4 tsps salt
1 tsp ground coriander
1/4 tsp ground black pepper
1/4 tsp cayenne pepper
1 pinch ground cardamom

Directions

1. Heat your waffle cooker.
2. Process the following with your food processor: cardamom, garbanzo beans, cayenne, egg whites, black pepper, cilantro, coriander, parsley, salt, cumin, and flour, and garlic
3. Process until you have a smooth mixture. Enter everything into a bowl.
4. Coat your iron with nonstick spray.
5. For 6 mins cook 1/4 C. of mixture. Continue with remaining mixture.
6. Enjoy warm.

HERBED
Beef Tenderloin Roast

Prep Time: 20 mins
Total Time: 45 mins

Servings per Recipe: 20
Calories	1.7
Fat	0 g
Cholesterol	0 mg
Sodium	58.4 mg
Carbohydrates	0.4 g
Protein	0.1 g

Ingredients

1 Beef Tenderloin
1/2 tsp pepper
1/2 tsp salt, go for more it you like
1 tbsp oregano
1 tbsp parsley
1/2 tbsp rosemary

1/2 tbsp thyme
1 pinch red pepper flakes
1 tsp dried garlic powder
1 tbsp dried onion flakes

Directions

1. Before you do anything set the oven to 450 F.
2. Discard the thin membrane in the tenderloin.. Cut it in half and tie each half with a kitchen twine.
3. Get a small bowl: Add the rest of the ingredients and mix them well. Massage the mix into the tenderloin halves. and place them on the rack of a roasting pan.
4. Pour some olive oil on them then cook them for 27 min or until it is done to your liking. Allow it to rest for 6 min then serve it warm.
5. Enjoy.

Russet
Roasted Beef Stew

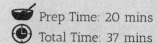 Prep Time: 20 mins
Total Time: 37 mins

Servings per Recipe: 4

Calories	165 kcal
Fat	3.6 g
Carbohydrates	23.8g
Protein	10.5 g
Cholesterol	18 mg
Sodium	390 mg

Ingredients

3 russet potatoes
2 C. 1/2-inch cubes roast beef
1 onion, finely chopped
1 green bell pepper, thinly sliced

1/2 C. sliced fresh mushrooms
1 tbsp vegetable oil

Directions

1. Make several holes in the potatoes with a fork and place them on an over proof plate. Microwave the potato for 9 min. Peel it and dice it.
2. Get a large bowl: Transfer the potato with beef and remaining veggies to it. Stir them.
3. Preheat a greased skillet. Lay in it the roast mix and cook them with stirring for 6 min. Turn over the mix and cook them for another 6 min.
4. Serve your stew warm.
5. Enjoy.

RUMP
Roast 101

Prep Time: 15 mins

Total Time: 8 hrs 15 mins

Servings per Recipe: 4

Calories	308 kcal
Fat	16.1 g
Carbohydrates	3.3g
Protein	35.3 g
Cholesterol	88 mg
Sodium	658 mg

Ingredients

3 lb rump roast
1 (10.75 oz) can condensed cream of
mushroom soup

1 (10.5 oz) can condensed beef broth

Directions

1. Get a slow cooker: Stir into it all the ingredients. Put on the lid and cook them for 8 h 30 min on low.
2. Serve your roast warm.
3. Enjoy.

Kosher Eye
Beef Roast

Prep Time: 5 mins
Total Time: 1 hr 5 mins

Servings per Recipe: 4
Calories	484 kcal
Fat	32.4 g
Carbohydrates	0.2g
Protein	44.8 g
Cholesterol	138 mg
Sodium	271 mg

Ingredients

3 lb beef eye of round roast
1/2 tsp kosher salt
1/2 tsp garlic powder

1/4 tsp freshly ground black pepper

Directions

1. Before you do anything set the oven to 375 F.
2. Tie the roast with a kitchen string. Sprinkle on it some salt, pepper and garlic powder.
3. Place the roast on a roasting pan and cook it for 1 h 10 min. Cover it with a piece of foil and let it stand for 17 min. Serve it warm.
4. Enjoy.

SOY SAUCE
Slow Cooker Beef Roast

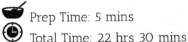

Prep Time: 5 mins
Total Time: 22 hrs 30 mins

Servings per Recipe: 6	
Calories	555 kcal
Fat	40.8 g
Carbohydrates	4.4g
Protein	40.4 g
Cholesterol	161 mg
Sodium	1369 mg

Ingredients

3 lb beef chuck roast
1/3 C. soy sauce
1 (1 oz) package dry onion soup mix

2 tsp freshly ground black pepper

Directions

1. Get a slow cooker: Stir in it the onion soup mix with soy sauce. Add the roast and cover it until it reaches 1/2 inch of the roast.
2. Stir in the black pepper and put on the lid. Cook the roast for 23 h. Serve it warm.
3. Enjoy.

Hash Brown Soup

Prep Time: 10 mins
Total Time: 35 mins

Servings per Recipe: 6

Calories	284 kcal
Fat	14 g
Carbohydrates	33.4g
Protein	7.7 g
Cholesterol	42 mg
Sodium	1112 mg

Ingredients

4 1/2 tbsps butter
1 1/2 C. frozen chopped onions
1 1/2 (14.5 oz.) cans chicken broth
1 (24 oz.) package frozen hash brown
potatoes (such as Ore-Ida(R) Steam n'
Mash(R)) Garlic Seasoned Potatoes)
3 tbsps all-purpose flour
1 1/2 tsps dried basil

3/4 tsp salt
3/4 tsp ground black pepper
3/4 tsp garlic salt
1 1/2 dashes hot sauce
1 (12 oz.) can evaporated milk

Directions

1. Stir fry your onions in butter for 7 mins then add in: the broth, hot sauce, potatoes, garlic salt, flour, pepper, basil and salt.
2. Get everything boiling, set the heat to low, and let the potatoes cook for 22 mins.
3. Add in the evaporated milk and stir the mix evenly.
4. Enjoy.

PARMESAN
Pepper Mashed Potatoes

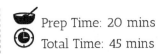 Prep Time: 20 mins
Total Time: 45 mins

Servings per Recipe: 6
Calories   301 kcal
Fat   16.1 g
Carbohydrates   32.3g
Protein   8.2 g
Cholesterol   45 mg
Sodium   231 mg

Ingredients

4 potatoes, peeled and cubed
1 tbsp extra-virgin olive oil
1/2 C. diced red bell pepper
1/2 C. diced yellow bell pepper
1/4 C. all-purpose flour
2 C. chicken broth
ground black pepper to taste
3 oz. baby spinach leaves

1/2 C. grated Parmesan cheese
2 tbsps bacon bits
1 tbsp minced garlic
2 tbsps butter
1/2 C. cream
salt and pepper to taste

Directions

1. Get your potatoes boiling in water and salt, set the heat to low, place a lid on the pot, and let everything cook for 22 mins.
2. Remove all the liquids and let the potatoes cool a bit.
3. Begin to stir fry your bell peppers in olive oil for 5 mins then add in the flour and continue cooking everything for 4 more mins.
4. Now add the broth and get everything boiling.
5. Let the mix cook for 17 mins then add some black pepper.
6. Remove the liquid from the potatoes then combine the spuds with: the garlic, baby spinach, bacon bits, and parmesan.
7. Begin to partially mash the potatoes then add in the cream and butter and mash the potatoes fully until smooth.
8. When serving the potatoes top them liberally with the gravy.
9. Enjoy.

Mashed Potatoes Bites

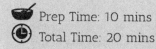 Prep Time: 10 mins
Total Time: 20 mins

Servings per Recipe: 6
Calories	556 kcal
Fat	25.7 g
Carbohydrates	34.8g
Protein	44.5 g
Cholesterol	139 mg
Sodium	945 mg

Ingredients

1/2 C. vegetable oil for frying
1 1/2 C. milk
1 egg
1 (7.6 oz.) package garlic flavored instant mashed potatoes

2 tsps salt
2 tsps ground black pepper
1 1/2 lbs chicken tenders

Directions

1. Get a bowl, combine: eggs and milk.
2. At the same time begin to get your oil hot.
3. Get a 2nd bowl and combine the potatoes with pepper and salt.
4. Coat your pieces of chicken with the milk mix then dredge the chicken in the dry mix.
5. Fry the chicken for 9 mins until browned on both sides.
6. Enjoy.

SOUR CREAM, Cheddar, and Mashed Potatoes

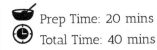 Prep Time: 20 mins
Total Time: 40 mins

Servings per Recipe: 8	
Calories	430 kcal
Fat	17 g
Carbohydrates	61.2g
Protein	10.8 g
Cholesterol	43 mg
Sodium	766 mg

Ingredients

7 large potatoes, peeled and cubed
1 (10 oz.) package frozen chopped
spinach, thawed and drained
1 C. sour cream
1/4 C. butter
2 tbsps chopped green onions

2 tsps salt
1/4 tsp black pepper
1 C. shredded Cheddar cheese

Directions

1. Coat a baking dish with oil then set your oven to 400 degrees before doing anything else.
2. Get your potatoes boiling in water and salt for 17 mins then remove the liquids and begin to partially mash the potatoes in a bowl.
3. Add in: the pepper, spinach, salt, sour cream, green onions, and butter.
4. Fully mash the potatoes until everything is smooth then spread the mix into the baking dish.
5. Cook the spuds in the oven for 17 mins then lay your cheese over everything. Let the potatoes cook for 7 more mins.
6. Enjoy.

Mashed Potatoes Noodles

🥣 Prep Time: 45 mins
🕐 Total Time: 1 hr 25 mins

Servings per Recipe: 8
Calories	336 kcal
Fat	18.4 g
Carbohydrates	35.2g
Protein	9.4 g
Cholesterol	0 mg
Sodium	1024 mg

Ingredients

1/4 C. chopped fresh green chile peppers
1 tbsp coarsely chopped garlic
2 tbsps fresh ginger, peeled and coarsely chopped
1 tsp salt
1/8 tsp ground turmeric
2 tsps vegetable oil
1 lb potatoes, peeled

3 C. water
3 1/2 C. chickpea flour
2 1/2 tsps salt
1 tsp ground turmeric
2 tbsps mustard oil
vegetable oil for deep frying

Directions

1. Place the following into the bowl of a food processor: 2 tbsps veggie oil, chilies, 1/8 tsp turmeric, garlic, 1 tsp salt, and ginger.
2. Process the mix until it is smooth.
3. Get your potatoes boiling in water and salt, set the heat to low, place a lid on the pot, and let everything cook for 17 mins.
4. Place the potatoes in a bowl and begin to mash them.
5. Try to get everything very smooth by adding in some of the water from boiling.
6. Add in 1 tbsp of green chili paste, mustard oil, chickpea flour, 1 tsp turmeric, 2.5 tsps of salt.
7. Then add in some more potato water and form a dough from the mix.
8. Now get your oil hot in a deep pan and use a potato ricer to fry noodles for 3 mins.
9. Fry all the potatoes in this manner.
10. Enjoy.

30-MINUTE
Mediterranean Chicken Soup

 Prep Time: 10 mins

Total Time: 30 mins

Servings per Recipe: 15
Calories	323 kcal
Fat	13.5 g
Carbohydrates	23.8g
Protein	24.4 g
Cholesterol	69 mg
Sodium	2011 mg

Ingredients

2 (48 oz.) containers chicken broth
4 (12 oz.) cans chicken chunks, drained
1 1/2 C. white rice
2 (26 oz.) cans cream of chicken soup

3/4 C. lemon juice

Directions

1. In a pan, add the chicken broth and canned chicken and bring to a boil.
2. Stir in the rice and simmer for about 15-20 minutes.
3. Stir in the cream of chicken soup and lemon juice and simmer for about 5-10 minutes, stirring occasionally.

Grocery
Rotisserie Orzo Chicken Soup

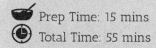 Prep Time: 15 mins
Total Time: 55 mins

Servings per Recipe: 5

Calories	514 kcal
Fat	11.4 g
Carbohydrates	70.4g
Protein	31.2 g
Cholesterol	65 mg
Sodium	1859 mg

Ingredients

2 (32 oz.) cartons chicken broth
1/2 cooked rotisserie chicken, meat removed from bones and chopped
1 C. sliced carrots
1 Macintosh apple, cored and diced
1/2 onion, diced

1/2 C. sliced celery
1/4 C. grated Parmesan cheese
1 bay leaf
2 C. orzo pasta

Directions

1. In a large pan, add the chicken broth, chicken, carrots, apple, onion, celery, Parmesan cheese and bay leaf and bring to a boil.
2. Reduce the heat to medium-low and simmer for about 30 minutes.
3. Stir in the orzo and cook for about 11 minutes, stirring occasionally.

UPSTATE NY
Inspired Chicken Soup

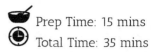 Prep Time: 15 mins

Total Time: 35 mins

Servings per Recipe: 8
Calories	294 kcal
Fat	21.5 g
Carbohydrates	8.1g
Protein	16.8 g
Cholesterol	78 mg
Sodium	863 mg

Ingredients

1/4 C. butter
3 stalks celery, diced
1 small onion, diced
1/4 C. all-purpose flour
2 C. chicken broth
1 C. water
3/4 C. half-and-half
2 C. cubed, cooked chicken

1 1/2 C. shredded Cheddar cheese
1/3 C. buffalo wing sauce
1/4 C. creamy tomato soup
Salt and ground black pepper to taste
1/4 C. crumbled blue cheese

Directions

1. In a large pan, melt the butter on medium-high heat and sauté the celery and onion for about 5 minutes.
2. Sprinkle flour over the soup and cook for about 2 minutes, stirring continuously.
3. Slowly, add the chicken broth, water and half-and-half, stirring continuously.
4. Stir in the Cheddar cheese, buffalo wing sauce and tomato soup and bring to a gentle boil, stirring occasionally.
5. Cook for about 10 minutes.
6. Serve hot with a topping of the blue cheese crumbles.

Chicken Soup

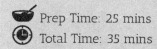
Prep Time: 25 mins
Total Time: 35 mins

Servings per Recipe: 4
Calories	288 kcal
Fat	13.9 g
Carbohydrates	22.9g
Protein	18.4 g
Cholesterol	59 mg
Sodium	1033 mg

Ingredients

3 C. chicken broth
2 cloves garlic, minced
1 1/2 tbsp unsalted butter
3/4 tsp white sugar
1 carrot, thinly sliced
1 stalk celery, thinly sliced
1 C. potato gnocchi
4 oz. frozen peas

4 oz. frozen corn
1 C. shredded cooked chicken
2 oz. baby spinach
Salt and freshly ground black pepper to taste
1/2 C. grated Parmesan cheese

Directions

1. In a large pan, add the broth, garlic, butter and sugar and bring to a gentle boil.
2. Cook for about 2 minutes.
3. Stir in the carrot and celery and bring to a boil.
4. Stir in the gnocchi and cook for about 2-3 minutes.
5. Add the peas and corn and cook for about 30 seconds.
6. Stir in the chicken, spinach, salt and black pepper and remove from the heat.
7. Serve hot with a topping of the Parmesan cheese.

SUNDAY'S
Spicy Chicken Ramen Noodle Soup

Prep Time: 10 mins
Total Time: 35 mins

Servings per Recipe: 4
Calories	165 kcal
Fat	8.5 g
Carbohydrates	6 g
Protein	16.5 g
Cholesterol	43 mg
Sodium	568 mg

Ingredients

2 tbsp sesame oil
1/2 tsp ground turmeric
2 tsp chopped fresh ginger root
2 tbsp chili paste
1 lb. chopped cooked chicken breast
1 quart chicken broth
2 tsp sugar
1/4 C. soy sauce

1 C. chopped celery
1 (3 oz.) package ramen noodles
1 C. shredded lettuce
1/2 C. chopped green onion

Directions

1. In a large pan, heat the oil on medium heat and sauté the turmeric, ginger and chili paste for about 1-2 minutes.
2. Stir in the chicken, broth, sugar, soy sauce and celery and bring to a boil.
3. Stir in the noodles and cook for about 3 minutes.
4. Stir in the lettuce and remove from the heat.
5. Serve with a garnishing of the green onions.

How to Make a Potato Salad Bavarian

Prep Time: 30 mins
Total Time: 50 mins

Servings per Recipe: 6
Calories	150.6
Fat	0.2g
Cholesterol	0.0mg
Sodium	402.4mg
Carbohydrates	33.1g
Protein	3.9g

Ingredients

1 medium onion, chopped
1 cucumber, sliced thinly
5 -6 radishes, sliced thin
3 tbsp all-purpose flour
2/3 C. cider vinegar

1 C. water
1 tsp salt
1/2 tsp ground pepper
6 -8 C. potatoes, sliced, cooked and peeled

Directions

1. In a pan, melt the butter and sauté the onion till tender.
2. Add the flour and stir to combine.
3. Add the cider vinegar and water and cook till the mixture becomes thick, stirring continuously.
4. In a large serving bowl, mix together the potato, radishes, cucumbers, salt and pepper.
5. Place the hot onion mixture over potato mixture and gently, stir to combine.
6. Serve immediately.

GERMAN
Dumplings

Prep Time: 15 mins
Total Time: 35 mins

Servings per Recipe: 1
Calories   189.2
Fat   5.1g
Cholesterol   74.5mg
Sodium   638.8mg
Carbohydrates   27.4g
Protein   7.7g

Ingredients

8 hard French rolls
2 eggs, whisked
1 C. whole milk, scalded

1 tsp kosher salt
1 large handful fresh parsley, chopped

Directions

1. Cut the bread into 1/4-inch thick slices.
2. In a large bowl, add the bread slices, eggs, parsley and kosher salt and mix well.
3. In a pan, add the milk and heat to till very hot but not boiling.
4. Add the milk over the bread mixture evenly.
5. With a towel, cover the bowl and keep aside for a few minutes.
6. With your hands, mix the bread mixture till just combined.
7. With wet hands, make 6 equal sized balls from the mixture and refrigerate to chill for about 15-30 minutes or overnight.
8. In a pan of salted boiling water, cook the dumplings for about 15-20 minutes.

Bavarian
Pineapple Shells

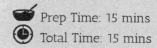

Prep Time: 15 mins
Total Time: 15 mins

Servings per Recipe: 1
Calories	2154.6
Fat	148.5g
Cholesterol	326.0mg
Sodium	1047.7mg
Carbohydrates	189.4g
Protein	23.8g

Ingredients

1/4 oz. unflavored gelatin
1/4 C. cold water
1 C. pineapple juice, unsweetened
1/4 C. sugar
3/4 C. mango puree

1 C. heavy cream, whipped
1 pie shell (regular cooked)

Directions

1. In a bowl, dissolve the gelatin in cold water and keep aside till softened.
2. In a medium pan, add the sugar and pineapple juice on medium heat and cook till the sugar is dissolved, stirring continuously.
3. In a large bowl, add the gelatin mixture, pineapple juice mixture and mango puree and beat till well combined.
4. Refrigerate the mixture till set partially.
5. Fold the whipped cream into mango puree mixture.
6. Place the mixture into the pie shell evenly and refrigerate to chill before serving.

BAVARIAN
Chocolate
Cheese Truffles

Prep Time: 15 mins
Total Time: 1 hr

Servings per Recipe: 24
Calories   224.9
Fat   11.9g
Cholesterol   15.5mg
Sodium   256.4mg
Carbohydrates   28.5g
Protein   3.0g

Ingredients

1 (18 1/4 oz.) boxes chocolate cake mix
2 (3 oz.) boxes raspberry Jell-O gelatin
12 oz. cream cheese, room temp
1 (12 oz.) frozen whipped topping,
thawed and divided

1/4 C. frozen raspberries
1/4 C. granulated sugar

Directions

1. Set your oven to 350 degrees F before doing anything else and grease and flour 11x15-inch jelly roll pans.
2. Prepare the cake mix according to package's instructions.
3. Divide the cake mixture into the prepared pans evenly and with the back of a spatula, smooth the surface.
4. Cook in the oven for about 15 minutes or till a toothpick inserted in the center of cakes comes out clean.
5. Remove from the oven and keep onto the wire rack to cool in the pan for about 5-10 minutes.
6. Carefully, invert the cakes onto the wire rack to cool completely.
7. In a bowl, dissolve the gelatin into 1 2/3 C. of the boiling water and keep aside for about 2 minutes.
8. In a food processor, add the cream cheese and pulse for about 1 minute.
9. Add the gelatin mixture and pulse for about 1 minute.
10. Transfer the gelatin mixture into a large bowl.
11. With a rubber spatula, gently fold in 4 C. of the whipped topping.
12. Place the gelatin mixture over each cake evenly and refrigerate to chill for about 15 minute.
13. Place 1 cake layer over second cake layer.

14. Spread remaining whipped topping on top of the cake evenly.
15. In a bowl, add the granulated sugar and roll the frozen raspberries in it.
16. Cut the cake into equal sized squares and top with the raspberries.

BAVARIAN
Veggie Soup

 Prep Time: 20 mins
Total Time: 1 hr 20 mins

Servings per Recipe: 8
Calories	187.4
Fat	9.0g
Cholesterol	22.9mg
Sodium	48.3mg
Carbohydrates	25.2g
Protein	3.9g

Ingredients

6 tbsp unsalted butter
4 carrots, cut into 3/8 inch thick rounds
salt & freshly ground black pepper
1/4 C. finely chopped fresh parsley leaves
1 large celery root, peeled and sliced 1/4 inch thick
1 parsley root, peeled and sliced 1/4 inch thick
4 leeks, split lengthwise, washed well, and sliced

1 small cauliflower, broken into florets
1/2 lb. sugar snap pea, tough strings removed
1/2 lb. green beans, ends trimmed and cut into 1 inch pieces
1/2 head savoy cabbage, damaged outer leaves discarded, cored, and thinly sliced
1 lb. potato, peeled and sliced 1/4 inch thick
1 1/2 C. water

Directions

1. In a large casserole, melt 3 tbsp of the butter on medium-high heat and remove from the heat.
2. In the bottom of the casserole, arrange the carrots in a layer and sprinkle with the salt, pepper and a little of the parsley.
3. Top with the layer of the celery root, followed by the layers of the parsley root, leeks, cauliflower florets, sugar snap pea, green beans, savoy cabbage and potato, sprinkling each layer with the salt, pepper and parsley.
4. Place the remaining 3 tbsp of the butter over the potatoes in the form of the dots.
5. Place the water over the vegetables.
6. Cover the casserole tightly and bring to a boil.
7. Reduce the heat to low and simmer for about 1 hour.

Bavarian
Coconut Truffles

🥣 Prep Time: 15 mins
🕐 Total Time: 8 hrs 15 mins

Servings per Recipe: 8
Calories	432.3
Fat	22.8g
Cholesterol	99.8mg
Sodium	139.5mg
Carbohydrates	52.6g
Protein	7.7g

Ingredients

1 1/2 tbsp gelatin
4 tbsp coconut milk
1 (14 oz.) cans sweetened condensed milk
1 C. coconut milk
1/2 C. sugar

4 egg yolks
1 crème fraîche, Alouette Cuisine
7 oz. shredded coconut (toasted)

Directions

1. In a bowl, dissolve the gelatin into 4 tbsp of the coconut milk. Keep aside to bloom.
2. In a pan, add the condensed milk and remaining coconut milk on medium-high heat and bring to a gentle boil.
3. In a bowl, add the sugar and egg yolks and beat well.
4. Add a small amount the hot milk mixture into the egg yolk mixture and beat well.
5. Slowly, add the egg yolk mixture into the milk mixture and cook for about 5-7 minutes, stirring continuously.
6. Remove from the heat and stir in the gelatin mixture.
7. Transfer the mixture into a bowl and refrigerate till the mixture begins to gel.
8. In another bowl, add the crème fraîche and beat till soft peaks form.
9. In the bowl of gel mixture, fold in crème fraiche.
10. Immediately, place the mixture into your favorite molds and refrigerate overnight.
11. Remove from the molds and serve with a topping of the shredded coconut.

BAVARIAN
Swedish Meatball

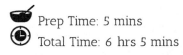

Prep Time: 5 mins
Total Time: 6 hrs 5 mins

Servings per Recipe: 10
Calories	40.6
Fat	0.0g
Cholesterol	0.0mg
Sodium	3.4mg
Carbohydrates	7.6g
Protein	0.2g

Ingredients

1 (6 - 8 oz.) bags frozen precooked meatballs, thawed
1 medium onion, sliced
1/4 C. brown sugar, packed

3 tbsp beef and onion soup mix
1 (12 oz.) bottles beer, optional

Directions

1. In a slow cooker, add all the ingredients and gently, stir to combine.
2. Set the crock pot on Low and cook, covered for about 5-6 hours.
3. Serve immediately.

Beef Rolls of Bacon, Onions, and Pickles (Rouladen Bavarian)

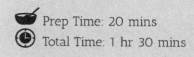 Prep Time: 20 mins
Total Time: 1 hr 30 mins

Servings per Recipe: 6

Calories	264 kcal
Fat	17.4 g
Carbohydrates	7.7g
Protein	19.1 g
Cholesterol	59 mg
Sodium	1450 mg

Ingredients

1 1/2 lbs flank steak, 1/4 inch fillets, 3 inches in width
German stone ground mustard, to taste
1/2 lb thick sliced turkey bacon
2 large onions, sliced

1 (16 oz.) jar dill pickle slices
2 tbsps butter
2 1/2 C. water
1 cube beef bouillon

Directions

1. Top each piece of steak with mustard then layer: onions, pickles, and bacon on each.
2. Shape the filet into a roll then place a toothpick in each to preserve the structure.
3. Brown your steaks in butter then add in 2.5 C. of water and bouillon.
4. Mix the bouillon and water together and then gently boil the rolls for 60 mins with a low level of heat.
5. Enjoy.

BAVARIAN
Empanadas

Prep Time: 20 mins
Total Time: 45 mins

Servings per Recipe: 6
Calories	674 kcal
Fat	42.3 g
Carbohydrates	32.5g
Protein	37.1 g
Cholesterol	114 mg
Sodium	894 mg

Ingredients

1/2 C. chopped onion
1 1/2 lbs lean ground beef
1 (16 oz.) can sauerkraut, drained and
pressed dry

2 (8 oz.) cans refrigerated crescent rolls
1 (8 oz.) package shredded Cheddar
cheese

Directions

1. Set your oven to 350 degrees before doing anything else.
2. Stir fry your beef and onions until the beef is fully done then remove all the excess oils before adding in your sauerkraut.
3. Get everything hot and then shut the heat.
4. Flatten your rolls and then place them into a casserole dish.
5. Top the rolls with the onion mix and then layer the 2nd piece of dough on top.
6. Crimp the edges of the two layers of dough together then top everything with some cheese.
7. Cook the dish in the oven for 27 mins.
8. Enjoy.

ENJOY THE RECIPES?
KEEP ON COOKING
WITH 6 MORE FREE COOKBOOKS!

Visit our website and simply enter your email address to join the club and receive your 6 cookbooks.

Printed in Great Britain
by Amazon